Winning Ways
for Early Childhood Professionals
Guiding Challenging Behavior

Gigi Schweikert

with Jeniece Decker
and Jennifer Romanoff

Name: _____

Date: _____

 Redleaf Press®
www.redleafpress.org
800-423-8309

Also in the Winning Ways series by Gigi Schweikert

Being a Supervisor
Being a Professional
Partnering with Families
Becoming a Team Player
Understanding Infants
Understanding Toddlers and Twos
Understanding Preschoolers
Supporting Positive Behavior
Responding to Behavior

Published by Redleaf Press
10 Yorkton Court
St. Paul, MN 55117
www.redleafpress.org

First edition 2016
Cover design by Jim Handrigan
Cover photograph by Dmitriy Shironosov / Hemera
Interior design by Wendy Holdman
Printed in the United States of America
23 22 21 20 19 18 17 16   1 2 3 4 5 6 7 8

Library of Congress Cataloging-in-Publication Data
Names: Schweikert, Gigi, 1962– author. | Decker, Jeniece, author. | Romanoff, Jennifer, author.
Title: Winning ways for early childhood professionals : guiding challenging behavior / Gigi Schweikert with Jeniece Decker and Jennifer Romanoff.
Description: First Edition. | St. Paul, MN : Redleaf Press, 2016.
Identifiers: LCCN 2016008428 | ISBN 9781605542294 (pbk.)
Subjects: LCSH: Problem children—Education (Early childhood) | Problem children—Behavior modification. | Early childhood teachers.
Classification: LCC LC4801 .S39 2016 | DDC 371.93—dc23
LC record available at https://lccn.loc.gov/2016008428

Printed on acid-free paper

Contents

From the Desk of Gigi Schweikert

Dear Winning Ways Reader
(and those desperate for a little "How do I get this child
to listen?" advice),

That's me doing what I love
most: working with children.

About the Authors

You may have noticed from the cover that for the
Winning Ways Behavior Series, I have teamed up with
two other passionate early childhood colleagues, Jennifer
Romanoff and Jeniece Decker. You'll learn more about
them throughout these books, and I am sure you will grow
to love them just as I do. Many years ago, Jim Greenman and Anne
Stonehouse invited me to join them as an author for the second edition of *Prime
Times.* Now it's my chance to do the same for Jennifer and Jeniece. Plus when it
comes to writing about children's behavior, I can use all the help I can get!

About the Book

Ever meet that one child—or a few—who never stops moving, always has a different idea in mind than you, and not only tests the limits but tests your limits? As a
parent, I have one of those children too. He's fourteen now, and he is still exploring
the world, taking things apart and putting them back together in a different way.
He's a thinker, a doer, a mover. Like my son, many of the children in your classroom are just too excited about exploring the world that we live in—they don't
have time to sit still and listen! They have their own agenda. Ultimately, to help
these children become successful, we'll need to help them balance their passion
for doing with their ability to get along with others, all while keeping that delicate
child spirit intact.

There will be children who need our help in other ways too. Perhaps they have
developmental delays or emotions triggered by environmental issues or events at
home. In these situations, we can love these children and their families well, and
we can seek the additional resources we need to help all children succeed, even the
most challenging ones!

Whether you're new to the field or a veteran early childhood educator, I think
you'll find the information in this Winning Ways book, *Guiding Challenging
Behavior,* helpful. We can all use a few more ideas!

After you finish reading the book, please e-mail us at gigi@gigischweikert.com with
your thoughts, ideas, and own stories about guiding challenging behavior. We'd
love to hear them.

Children deserve our winning ways,

Introduction

What's *Guiding Challenging Behavior* All About?

Welcome to the Winning Ways book *Guiding Challenging Behavior*. This is one of three books in the continuing series that includes *Supporting Positive Behavior, Responding to Behavior,* and *Guiding Challenging Behavior.* You can read all three or work with the one that best equips you as an early childhood professional.

This workbook is designed to help you do the following:

- Develop a better understanding of the behavior of children in child care
- Improve your response to challenging behavior
- Understand how to observe and help children with challenging behavior become successful

What Are Challenging Behaviors?

Learning to behave is a tremendous challenge, full of complexities and confusing messages. Young children strive for understanding, independence, connection, belonging, acknowledgment, and self-control. They learn by exploring, experimenting, testing the limits of their environment, and experiencing the consequences of their behavior. Through these learning experiences, children begin to understand how the world works, what their own limits are, and how to regulate their own behavior. Learning to behave is a big job that even some adults haven't mastered. For young children, this journey of self-control has only just begun. This book will help you guide children on their journey and show you what you can do to support them along their way. So much harder than arts and crafts!

Who Should Read and Use *Guiding Challenging Behavior?*

Guiding Challenging Behavior is intended for anyone who works in early childhood education:

Veteran educators Those who have seen every behavior imaginable over the years, have the patience of angels, and never tire of bringing the excitement and necessary routine to the classroom that children need to behave positively. With all the technology and the immediate gratification of the world we live in, you may be starting to scratch your head for some new ideas.

New teachers Those who have just started working with young children and never realized small children climb on almost everything and often push others to get the things they want. Sometimes, after a long day at work, you wonder, *Will I go back tomorrow?*

Career seekers Those who are considering becoming early childhood educators. The field needs trained, enthusiastic, active individuals. Is that you?

College students Those who are students in an early childhood program in a college or university.

Trainers Early childhood professionals who facilitate seminars and workshops.

Professors Those who teach adult students in early childhood education programs in colleges and universities.

Program supervisors Directors and other administrators who want to better support and train the staff in their programs.

Stressed-out teachers Those who are burning out or giving in and need some new ideas and encouragement because "these kids are driving me nuts."

Parents Parents of young children who, in today's busy world, often give in to their children's demands. They want and need support and advice on guiding their children and dealing with behavioral issues.

How Do You Use *Guiding Challenging Behavior?*

Guiding Challenging Behavior is divided into nine chapters. These can be read straight through, or you can select a chapter that helps with a specific issue for which you need guidance. Although reading the entire book will give you the greatest insight into guiding challenging behavior, each chapter stands alone as an educational or training tool. Here's what the book covers:

1 Identify Challenging Behavior

2 Establish a Successful Environment

3 Evaluate Your Teaching Methods

4 Observe, Observe, Observe!

5 Observe and Understand Challenging Behaviors

6 Create an Action Plan as a Team

7 Manage Difficult Conversations with Parents

8 Identify Additional Child Services

9 Find the Place Where the Child Can Be Most Successful

Is *Guiding Challenging Behavior* Intended for Group or Individual Use?

Either way works great! You can use *Guiding Challenging Behavior* as a training tool to work with a group or on your own. Whether you are working on your own or in a training group, read through the appropriate chapter and complete the exercises throughout the chapter and at the end. Jotting down your answers will give you the greatest benefit from the workbook. Also, if you are in a training group, having a written answer to refer to often makes you feel more comfortable sharing your thoughts during your actual meeting.

DESIGN

How Is *Guiding Challenging Behavior* Designed for Training?

The workbook is designed so that you will achieve the following:

- Experience active learning by participating in discussions, solving problems, and applying your new knowledge to your current work situation, and become reenergized about working in the early childhood field

- Connect your current knowledge with the new material and have opportunities to talk about and share common concerns and issues regarding team building

- Gain practical knowledge and tips that you can begin using in your program immediately

How to Use *Guiding Challenging Behavior* in Trainings

You can use the workshop presentation for a variety of training needs and situations. Here are some examples:

- Group of teachers in one classroom
- Administrators
- Lunch and learn
- Staff meeting
- In-service day
- Partnership of several programs
- Community outreach
- Recruiting tool
- Local conference

SELF-ASSESSMENT

How Are You Currently Guiding Challenging Behavior?

Complete the following assessment to see how you're currently guiding challenging behavior. Be honest with yourself. No single method for guiding children's behaviors works for everyone—we each have a slightly different approach. Assessing your knowledge, expectations, and environment is an important first step to guiding behavior positively.

How Well Do I Guide Children's Challenging Behavior?

1 I understand appropriate child behavior and can identify challenging behavior in my classroom.

> Always   Usually   Sometimes   Never

2 I create an ordered, flexible environment to help children succeed.

> Always   Usually   Sometimes   Never

3 When I encounter challenging behavior, I evaluate whether my approach and expectations are realistic.

> Always   Usually   Sometimes   Never

4 I regularly observe my classroom and each child to understand the behaviors in the classroom.

> Always   Usually   Sometimes   Never

5 When I have challenging behavior in my classroom, I complete specific observations to better understand and help those children and situations.

> Always   Usually   Sometimes   Never

6 After observing challenging behavior, I work with my team to determine patterns and issues and create an action plan for those children.

> Always   Usually   Sometimes   Never

7 I prepare for and carefully handle difficult conversations with parents about their children's challenging behavior.

> Always   Usually   Sometimes   Never

8 I support parents with additional services and resources to help children with behavioral challenges.

> Always   Usually   Sometimes   Never

9 I know my limits as an early childhood professional, and I support parents and children in finding the best place to ensure their success.

> Always   Usually   Sometimes   Never

Nine Steps to Guide Challenging Behavior

Refer back to your completed self-assessment while you explore the nine steps to guide challenging behavior. Whether you are on your own and reading and working at your leisure or training with a small group, you'll gain practical information you can use in the classroom and techniques to support the positive behavior of young children. Let's get started!

guiding challenging behavior

1

Identify Challenging Behavior

I understand appropriate child behavior and can identify challenging behavior in my classroom.

- Always
- Usually
- Sometimes
- Never

What's the Difference between Challenging Behavior and Developmentally Appropriate Behavior?

An early childhood classroom is full of children with unique personalities and behaviors. You will see lots of "I can't believe that child just did that" behavior, and sometimes it's easy to confuse challenging behavior with some common, developmentally appropriate behaviors. But what's the difference?

Developmentally appropriate behaviors These are behaviors you expect to see as children are typically developing. Developmentally appropriate behavior varies by age group. For example, many toddlers bite. The behavior is developmentally appropriate because toddlers have a limited ability to express themselves verbally. The behavior is still unacceptable.

Challenging behaviors These are behaviors that children exhibit consistently and that often require attention beyond that of typical behavior. Challenging behavior can potentially harm adults, other children, or the child displaying it. Challenging behavior also disrupts any learning environment or interferes with successful learning.

Sometimes developmentally appropriate behaviors are also disruptive and challenging. On some days, toddlers who pushed chairs was challenging for me (Gigi) as a teacher. But many times, behaviors you think are challenging are really just children behaving like children, doing exactly what they should be doing at their stages of development. If you can understand the difference between the two, you'll have a much better handle on what to expect from children and how to guide challenging behavior. Let's look at some of the different stages of developmentally appropriate behavior.

Infants

When infants first begin to move around, they seem to relate to other young children not as people but as interesting objects to explore. Infants will display behaviors like:

Poking They'll push their own fingers into their friends' mouths or even yours to see what happens. At times you may see them trying to pull their friends' fingers into their own mouths!

Climbing They climb over friends or furniture as if they are toys because they are still learning about their surroundings. These climbing babies aren't intentionally trying to hurt other children—they are just on the move.

Mouthing This is a method of exploring their worlds. If infants chew crayons, eat dough when they manipulate it, or suck on paintbrushes, they are probably not yet developmentally ready for these materials.

Touching They touch everything with no sense of property rights. Infants don't understand sharing, and they are likely to take toys from others.

As infants explore, they don't realize that it's okay to tug on their stuffed animals' hair but that tugging on the hair of a friend sitting next to them is not. You can redirect infants to things they can poke, touch, and climb over. Use redirection statements like "Sara's skin feels soft; touch her gently like this," or "Miss Gigi's hair is long, but it hurts me when you pull on it. Here's a toy you can pull." (See the Winning Ways book *Responding to Behavior* for more ideas on guiding and redirecting.) If these love shoves and rough hugs become increasingly strong or more consistent, or if they can't be redirected, then you may have a challenging behavior.

What types of behaviors have you seen infants exhibit that aren't listed above?

_____

_____

Based on the behaviors you listed, at what age can these expected behaviors, or developmentally appropriate behaviors, turn into challenging behaviors?

_____

Toddlers

Most of the frustrating toddler behaviors are still developmentally appropriate—you should expect them from toddlers in your care. Even a seasoned toddler teacher may need a little help on some days. Here are some behaviors you can expect from toddlers.

Asserting their autonomy Shouting "*Mine!*" every few minutes. Toddlers simply want independence! When toddlers are uncooperative, even defiant, they need gentle guidance, reasonable limits, and a teacher who understands the difficulty they have asserting their newly found independence. Redirection is key. Getting frustrated and angry with a toddler only leaves the two of you with *two* temper tantrums—and it's only developmentally appropriate for one of you.

Being active and curious about the world Toddlers are constantly on the move, touching everyone and everything! It's easy to label some investigative toddlers as aggressive, but that's rarely the case. Most toddlers are just exploring the world, and that means exploring other toddlers too.

Becoming social scientists in their relationships In a toddler room, you will see casual pushes, smacks, or pokes of one toddler to another, often motivated by a desire to see what will happen next. Toddlers may set out to achieve a goal, like getting toys back from other children, without understanding the consequences of their actions—for example, accidentally hurting another child.

Most of the hurtful things toddlers do are just a result of their developmental stage. However, when they constantly hurt others or have many tantrums a day, they may need additional support with their challenging behaviors.

What other behaviors do you see toddlers demonstrate?

_____

_____

Based on the behaviors you listed, when can these expected or developmentally appropriate behaviors turn into challenging behaviors?

_____

_____

Preschoolers

By preschool age, children's behaviors appear more intentional. Preschoolers are becoming social beings. They are interested in exploring the world and interacting with others. They are just learning to take turns, share, and resolve conflict. Here are some behaviors you may see from preschoolers.

Physically hurting others Preschoolers may hit or kick to accomplish a particular goal. These may be challenging behaviors to you, but they are also developmentally appropriate while preschoolers begin to develop conflict resolution skills.

Whining This is an immature but developmentally appropriate way for preschoolers to express their wants and needs. Young children are more likely to whine when they are tired because effective communication requires effort and energy. When preschoolers whine more than they talk, you can help them learn to express their wants by asking questions, pointing, or just slowing down.

Testing limits and challenging rules With preschoolers, you'll start to hear "But why?" and find yourself negotiating with them quite a bit. Preschoolers love to see exactly how far they can get as they learn about boundaries and expectations. However, this becomes a challenging behavior when this testing and rule breaking puts children or others in danger.

What additional behaviors do you see preschoolers exhibit?

_____

_____

You may be thinking these are the challenging behaviors you see in your classroom every day! Remember, the behaviors described above for infants, toddlers, and preschoolers are developmentally appropriate. This is just what children do! But that doesn't mean these behaviors are okay. You still need to redirect the children to behaving appropriately. Your job as an early childhood teacher is to help children learn to interact with the world. And right now their world is your classroom. When children's behaviors are disruptive in the classroom or are hurtful to themselves, others, or property, then those are challenging behaviors. Let's talk more about what challenging behavior can look like.

guiding challenging behavior

Understanding Challenging Behaviors

Challenging behavior is defined as repetitive behavior that harms children themselves, others, or property. To understand challenging behavior, you need to understand what is developmentally appropriate behavior for each age. For example, toddlers' understanding of language far outweighs their actual verbal abilities. This means that some toddlers cannot express their thoughts and feelings in verbally effective ways. Think about how frustrating that would be: You need to get your point across, but you've lost your voice. You point, make grunting noises, and *no one* understands you! The scope of certain behaviors can also determine whether they are challenging behaviors. How often is the behavior present, and on what scale does it occur? Is a child biting *every day*, or is the biting sporadic? Do they all go crazy once circle time is over? Understanding behavior patterns is as important as understanding the behaviors themselves.

Challenging Behaviors in Your Classroom

Reflect on some of the challenging behaviors you've seen in your classroom. Is it one specific child? Is it all of them? Is it a specific time of day? Without naming names, make a list of the behaviors you see that you consider challenging.

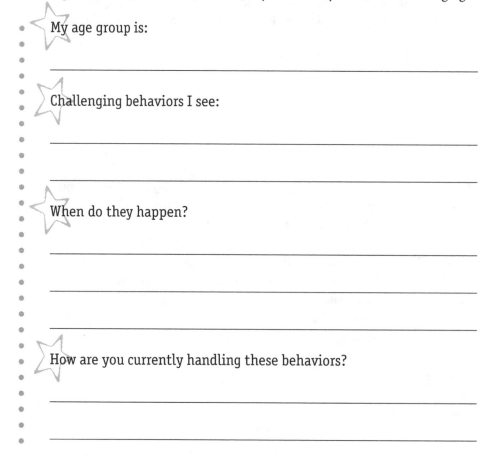

My age group is:

_____

Challenging behaviors I see:

_____

_____

When do they happen?

_____

_____

_____

How are you currently handling these behaviors?

_____

_____

Typical Challenging Behavior

Challenging behaviors can be anything that disrupts your classroom or hurts others, but you will typically see a few common ones in your early childhood classroom. These are some typical challenging behaviors children may demonstrate in your program:

Infants
- Biting
- Temper tantrums (often includes a combination of crying, screaming, kicking, and lying on the floor)

Toddlers
- Anger (throwing, kicking, hitting, spitting)
- Temper tantrums (often includes a combination of crying, screaming, kicking, and lying on the floor)
- Biting
- Whining

Preschool
- Tattling
- Answering back (assertive tone of voice and/or body language)
- Noncompliance with rules or boundaries
- Inappropriate language
- Inappropriate play (violent play or inappropriate touching of children or adults)

One of the main reasons these challenging behaviors get *repeated* is because they receive strong reactions from other children and adults. But do you know what makes these behaviors happen in the first place? Let's break it down:

Challenging Behavior	Why might it be happening?
Biting	Lack of communication skills, frustration, lack of impulse control, teething
Temper tantrums (crying, screaming, kicking, and lying on the floor)	Lack of emotional control, frustration, not getting what they want, learned behavior due to positive reinforcement (*Grandma gives in every time!*)
Anger (kicking, hitting, spitting)	Lack of maturity, frustration, instigated by a conflict, lack of emotional control, lack of communication skills
Whining	Tired, hungry, lack of language
Tattling	Seeking approval, behavior that is reinforced (mom uses child routinely to spy and divulge what siblings are doing)
Answering back	Lack of vocabulary, strong willed, lack of emotional response or control over emotional expression
Inappropriate language	Attention seeking, reinforced behavior (*Dad thinks it's funny! Why don't you?*), spontaneous use because they have overheard it

guiding challenging behavior

On page 14, you wrote down the challenging behaviors you see in your classroom. Are any of the common behaviors above on your list? You can recognize and help children avoid these reactions and behaviors better if you know the reasons behind them. Refer to the Winning Ways book *Supporting Positive Behavior* to learn what you can do to help children avoid or at least minimize these common behaviors.

My First Lightbulb Moment: Thoughts from Jeniece

I was new to being a lead teacher in an older toddler classroom when we moved a class of younger toddlers, including Emily, who had bitten several times. Emily's biting was difficult to track—never at the same time and never the same children. But what I did notice about Emily was that she didn't talk very much. Emily liked to point and was quite possessive of her things. I encouraged Emily over and over to use her words.

After a few biting incidents, I sat with Emily one-on-one and discussed how important it was for her to use her words to tell her friends or me how she felt. It was the first time I saw her face light up a little with acknowledgment. Later that same day, Emily was sitting, preparing a meal for herself and her doll in the dramatic play area. Jason came over and started swiping the dishes away. She put one hand down on the plate and said, "No!" He went for the cup; she threw her other arm down and said, "Stop!" He went for the doll, and because both her hands were occupied saving the plate and cup, all she had left was . . . her mouth! She went in for the bite, but I had heard her from across the room, and I was able to stop her before she made contact.

Emily had used all the words she could at her age, and Jason clearly was not listening. She felt helpless and resorted to biting. I helped retrieve the things she was desperately trying to save and thanked her for not only using her words but also using them *loudly* so that I could come help. She smiled, we hugged, and she continued having her meal with her doll. Over time Emily began verbally communicating more and more—and she never bit in my class again.

A Call for Help: Red Flag Behavior

Red flag behaviors make you stop and look more closely at the child's actions. Does the child need more help than you can provide? You are skilled at teaching young children and helping facilitate their learning, and that includes helping children with socialization, guidance, and self-regulation. Sometimes you may see red flag behavior that just doesn't feel right to you. You may not know what it is, but you have that feeling. Go with it! It's better to be wrong than to have missed an opportunity to help a child. Most of you are not qualified or licensed to diagnose children's behavior. Your role is to help children succeed as much as you can in your group setting, to observe and document their behavior, to work with your center administrators to reach out to the parents, and eventually as a program-parent team, to get children the diagnosis and help they need.

Remember that a behavior or diagnosis does not define a child. Some may have a special need that results in their challenging behavior—for example, an inability to calm themselves, distractibility, aggressive behavior, or hyperactivity. The principles for helping these children succeed in the classroom setting are the same as for other, more typical children: understand the child, partner with the parents to determine what works best, adapt the setting, and keep the special need in perspective.

What to Look For:
Possible Developmental Red Flag Behaviors

Teachers who have a good grasp of child development often pick up on children's developmental red flags. The behaviors listed below are considered red flag behaviors. Stop, pause, and see if the behavior (or lack of a behavior) indicates a need beyond redirection and other guidance techniques. As with challenging behaviors, red flag behaviors seen once or twice do not indicate an immediate problem. Even children can have a bad day! But when these behaviors are consistent or clearly disrupt children's ability to socialize and learn, you need to alert your center's administrator, who may involve the child's parents to seek other experts.

- No eye contact
- Lack of emotion
- Inappropriate expression of emotion
- No acknowledgment when called or spoken to
- Preoccupation with tasks
- Difficulty switching tracks
- Aggression
- Withdrawal

guiding challenging behavior

➤ Stop and Pause:
Identifying Red Flag Behaviors

Have you seen any of these red flag behaviors in your classroom?

Yes   No

If so, how were they handled?

_____

Go With Your Gut!

It is easy to lose perspective if red flag behaviors are present and you don't feel equipped to help the child succeed. Children should not be defined by their behavior or special needs. Early childhood professionals have to avoid the inappropriate, but understandable, *they-don't-belong-in-my-group* attitude.

In these situations, you should always go with your gut. Does the behavior you've observed seem more than usually challenging or different? You should know the children in your classroom well. You spend a great deal of time with them. The longer you work with the same age group, the easier it is to spot behavior that may seem different. This doesn't necessarily mean something is wrong, but you know that it's time to talk to your director and ask for help yourself. Together you can decide the best next steps.

Early childhood classrooms are full of learning, fun, and laughter. Each classroom hosts many different personalities and unique qualities. Each child comes with unique perspectives and different behaviors. Knowing how to spot developmentally appropriate behaviors and how to differentiate them from challenging behaviors will ensure that all of the children get the care and education they need. The next chapter focuses on the environment. How you structure your classroom can help or hinder how a child behaves. Ready to consider a classroom makeover?

winning ways

OPTIMIZE YOUR KNOWLEDGE

1. Explain why a developmentally appropriate behavior may still be an inappropriate behavior.

   _____

   _____

   _____

2. Why is it important to understand what causes children to behave in certain ways?

   _____

   _____

   _____

3. Think of a child in your program who exhibits a challenging behavior. Can you suggest a reason why the behavior might occur?

   _____

   _____

   _____

4. Describe a red flag behavior you have encountered in your classroom.

   _____

   _____

   _____

2 Establish a Successful Environment

I create an ordered, flexible environment to help children succeed.

- Always
- Usually
- Sometimes
- Never

It's a Complex World

What's it like to be a child just learning the rules? Imagine you are driving in a world without traffic lights and signs. The roads have no lanes and the parking lots have no marked spaces. Yet the police expect you to follow these complicated rules, and they often ask you to do things you don't fully understand. When you mess up, they punish you and create new rules. Don't you think it might be the same for children as they navigate their complex new world? Think about it this way. When children "misbehave," they are really just doing what they want to do. Isn't doing what you want a wonderful feeling? Many times teachers tell children "No" or "Don't do that," and children must be thinking, *But why? I want to. Tell me why I can't!* It takes time to help children understand socialization and guidance.

Does Your Environment Set Children Up to Fail?

When you observe challenging behaviors, it's important to ask yourself, *Am I setting children up to behave this way?* The environment plays a huge part in how children behave. Think about the difference between a child who's a perfect little angel at home versus the one who erupts in the toy aisle at a store. It's hard to believe, but yes, it's the same child. It's easy to blame the child for challenging behaviors, but before you go there, take a look at the child's environment.

LET'S TRY TO RELATE

When I (Jeniece) visited a busy superstore during the holiday season, I saw toys and clothes on the floor, displays disorganized, a few people fighting loudly, and the rest of the store dirty because of the holiday sales rush. What are your feelings when you leave a store like this? I, for sure, am moody, annoyed, and just can't wait to get out. But I feel good when I walk into other stores where I am greeted by an employee and am offered a yummy sample from the cookie tray or a nice spray of perfume and see all the items displayed attractively. I leave with a breath of fresh air and a big smile, and feeling a little pampered.

Think about the differences between these two experiences. Have you ever felt the difference? Well, that's exactly how your classroom environment affects children. If your room is an unattractive, chaotic mess, how do you expect children to behave? It is likely the children will react with chaotic, messy behaviors. The way your room is set up and the schedule that you follow can have a lot to do with the behaviors you see.

Observe from a Child's Perspective

Observe your environment to see how it affects children's behavior. Get down at a child's level. See what the children see. You can really see your classroom through the eyes of a child.

For infants: lie on your belly and look around.
What do you see?

_____

_____

For toddlers: sit on your backside and look around.
What do you see?

_____

_____

For preschoolers: sit up on your knees and look around.
What do you see?

_____

_____

guiding challenging behavior

Once you've observed your classroom from child height, experience the classroom from children's perspective. Play with the toys you have in your room. Put yourself in the children's mind-set. Would you be interested? Would you be you engaged? If the answer is no, what could you do to ensure that the environment is engaging? You could add more exciting toys or ensure that the toys are all in working condition and have all their pieces. Preventing some challenging behavior may be as simple as replacing the puzzle with the missing piece that has been driving Samir crazy because he just can't finish it!

What Makes a Successful Environment?

Your environment is much more than just its physical space and setup. Schedules, transitions, equipment, even a child's comfort level make up the environment or feel of the room. Look at each aspect to understand how it affects the children's experiences.

What Do You Want Children to Do?

Most early childhood programs promote children's independence, autonomy, self-esteem, and self-care, as well as care for others and the physical environment. The basis for achieving these goals is a secure, orderly, developmentally appropriate environment—a positive, "yes" environment that allows children to experiment and test their behavior within clearly defined limits.

What are some of the goals for your classroom or program?

_____

_____

How does your environment support those goals?

_____

_____

How does your environment hinder those goals?

_____

_____

winning ways

WHAT MAKES A SUCCESSFUL ENVIRONMENT?

Whatever your program goals may be, successful environments share some common characteristics. Do you have a successful environment?

- Realistic expectations for children's self-control
- Enough open, but structured, space
- Enough materials and proper equipment
- Developmentally appropriate materials and equipment
- Flexible routines
- Flexible spaces
- Flexible schedule
- Teachers with a positive attitude
- Order and predictability
- Free of temptations—that is, few objects and places that are forbidden
- Quiet learning areas
- Realistic and developmentally appropriate requirements for sharing
- Little waiting
- Routines without frequent periods of sitting still
- Hands-on, active learning
- Child-directed activity
- Consistent responses from adults
- Limited teacher-directed activity in which children are expected to only look and listen for long periods of time (How long is too long? Check out *Supporting Positive Behavior*, one of the other books in this Winning Ways series.)

Routine and Schedule

Schedule and routine go hand in hand with the physical environment. Young children like a predictable environment. Preschoolers and even older toddlers will catch you if you try to skip any part of your routine. They'll even catch you if you miss a page in a book! Any change in routine is often hard for children. Their behavior can be drastically different if Daddy drops them off in the morning when Mommy normally does.

Your life is all about time. *What time do I have to go to work? Can I sleep a few more minutes? When does the movie start?* Children have no sense of time, but they do understand sequence, or the routine or order of the day. They will recognize when you do not sing the circle time "Good-bye Song," but they won't recognize that it is 10:20 and free play was supposed to end at 10:15. Children will know your routine based on a "First this, then that" perspective.

Flexibility

Physical flexibility is a must in early childhood education, from up on your toes to down on your knees, but you must be cognitively flexible too. *Cognitive flexibility* means that you can see when your plans for children just aren't working and can change them accordingly. You need this flexibility for the times when children are likely to have challenging behaviors. When the children are not engaged in the art project you planned, you need to stop it and switch to something that does engage them. Can you change your mind-set and plans when you see that something isn't working?

Are You Flexible? Self-Assessment

1 I get aggravated when I'm not on time according to the class schedule.

Always   Usually   Sometimes   Never

2 My whole day is thrown off when the schedule gets interrupted for a special event.

Always   Usually   Sometimes   Never

3 I can quickly think of something to entertain the children if we are made to wait.

Always   Usually   Sometimes   Never

4 If an art project is not going according to plan, I scrap it and have children freely draw with crayons.

Always   Usually   Sometimes   Never

5 I'm annoyed when an extra child comes to school on my low numbers day.

Always   Usually   Sometimes   Never

Think about your answers. How can you adjust your flexibility to accommodate the situation in each of your five answers? Even if you're one of the most flexible teachers, consider how you can positively affect your environment in each of these areas.

1 _____

2 _____

3 _____

4 _____

5 _____

winning ways

6 Ways to Stay Flexible

Try these guidelines to adopt more flexibility throughout the day:

1 Know when it's not working. Stop or change the activity if no one is participating. Get up and have a game of freeze dance if all the children have ants in their pants.

2 Attend to children's cues, leads, and communications. Use the same materials they are interested in; imitate their actions and sounds; comment on their choices, gestures, and expressions; or interpret their communications to one another.

3 Allow continuity when possible. Help children exit the group as needed (to get their diaper changed, use the bathroom, lie down on a cot), and keep activities going for the children who remain, or let children stay with what they choose.

4 Include a variety of choices. Provide a range of activities to engage or entertain children, such as books, sorting objects for each child, art materials, small- and large-motor manipulatives.

5 Plan your schedule according to the children's energy levels: music and movement after snack, story time before nap. You get it!

6 Anticipate. There will be tantrums and meltdowns and hits and bites, but doing your best to prevent them will do exactly that— prevent them!

Schedules and Transitions

Most classroom schedules should be used as a loose guide. Just because art time ends at 10:30 does not mean you should be pulling the paintbrushes out of William's hands at 10:29. Remember: everything a child does is a learning process. If you're rushing to finish, you just taught William that moving everyone to outside time is more important to you than allowing him to finish his creative masterpiece. Imagine if you were just about to push the send button on an e-mail, and a teacher said, "E-mail time is over. You can Send that e-mail tomorrow." What would you do? Probably push the Send button really quick! If William is upset to the point that he begins to act out later on, you might initially think it's for no reason, when in reality he just wanted to finish his painting, just as you wanted to send that e-mail.

guiding challenging behavior

Moving to the Next Activity: It's Over

Children need prompting when something is ending. As adults, we experience these kinds of cues throughout our daily experiences. We are so used to these cues that we sometimes take them for granted. We all know what a yellow light means—it means red is coming next. The yellow light is a transition cue for adults. Think about how chaotic driving would be without a yellow light. But how many of us speed through the yellow light so we don't get stuck at a red? A classroom without proper transitions is an intersection without yellow lights. Yikes! To prevent situations that may lead to unwanted or challenging behaviors, you must provide strong transition cues.

What about Your Schedule?

Think about your schedule and pinpoint when your most difficult times are. What type of transitions could help you during these times? List them below.

_____

_____

_____

_____

_____

You can create a successful learning environment if you give yourself time to review your current space. Children need space, but what that space is filled with is just as important. Remember that children explore every bit of space you provide them. Make sure their environment is worth exploring and that it sets them up for success! Next, you'll reflect on your teaching methods and how you can help improve the behavior in your classroom.

OPTIMIZE YOUR KNOWLEDGE

1 What small change will you make in your environment today to make it more successful tomorrow?

_____

_____

_____

_____

2 Describe a situation in the past in which you could have been more flexible.

_____

_____

_____

_____

3 In what ways will you improve your transitions going forward?

_____

_____

_____

_____

guiding challenging behavior

3

Evaluate Your Teaching Methods

When I encounter challenging behavior, I evaluate whether my approach and expectations are realistic.

- ○ Always
- ○ Usually
- ○ Sometimes
- ○ Never

The Blame Game

When you hit a frustration point with challenging behaviors, it's easy to try to find someone or something else to blame. *It's the parents! This child is just out of control! The babysitter is spoiling them!* It's not easy to admit that the problem might be you. Yes, you. You may be doing something or saying things that aggravate the child's behavior. It's hard to imagine, but teachers cause as many challenging behaviors as they try to solve. But this doesn't mean that the things you are doing are necessarily wrong. Instead, use challenging behaviors as opportunities to evaluate your discipline style and expectations of young children. To understand your role in children's behavior, you can examine your

- discipline style,
- classroom management,
- classroom environment,
- expectations of the children, and
- teaching and rule-making style.

It may sound like a lot, but these are all part of tasks you do every day, whether you know it or not. Let's get started!

Check Your Discipline Style

In the same way that everyone learns differently, everyone disciplines differently. You probably don't have the same style of discipline as your assistant teachers or a child's parent. But children learn best when everyone takes the same approach. Some people get loud when they discipline, some prefer time-outs, and others stick to positive reinforcement. Getting loud and time-outs are not appropriate for early childhood settings. Many times the methods you use to correct children's behavior can actually have a negative effect. Here are a few types of discipline styles. Let's take a look at each of them.

THE POWER APPROACH

When teachers use the power approach to discipline, it includes methods such as the following:

Yelling and raised voices toward the children You may feel you need to be loud to emphasize your points, but this method backfires. As an adult, you get quiet and lean in to listen when a presenter speaks softly; when a presenter has a loud voice and a microphone, you feel more comfortable having a side chat with a friend. The same applies in your classroom.

Attacking children's self-esteem Statements like "Boys don't cry" or "Do you want to go to the baby room?" are verbally and emotionally abusive and shaming. This type of discipline is never okay anytime from anyone.

Asking questions that aren't really questions Sometimes you ask children questions that you already know the answer to. "Have you finished cleaning up?" isn't a real question when a child is clearly still playing with toys on the floor. When you set children up to fail you, you can crush their self-esteem. They want to please you!

THE PERMISSIVE APPROACH

When teachers use the permissive discipline style, it often looks like this:

Avoiding discipline actions Permissive-style teachers don't want to deal with conflict or redirect children, and they use common phrases such as "Boys will be boys" or "All children do that at this age."

Fear of being the "bad guy" Permissive-style teachers do not want children to dislike them or get angry because they are being redirected or guided to more positive behavior.

Reacting against how you were disciplined as a child Some of you may have had parents or teachers who used the power approach, and you've vowed never to do that to a child. But in your attempts to avoid this disciplinary style, you may misguide children rather than help them.

guiding challenging behavior

THE INTERACTIVE APPROACH

The interactive discipline style, when you do it well, avoids the pitfalls of the power or permissive approaches and puts children on a path to learn self-control. The interactive approach involves the following:

Setting limits and defining consequences You make it clear to the children which behaviors are acceptable and which are not. You lay out the consequences for unacceptable behavior, and you follow through when necessary.

Acknowledging children's behavior You include children in the creation of classroom rules. You talk to them individually and on their level. You apply the techniques of redirection, and you help guide and shape behavior through positive reinforcement.

Consistency You have a clear, consistent approach about expectations, the ways you speak to children, and the ways in which children are redirected.

How Were You Disciplined as a Child?

Some of you may not want to think about some parts of your childhood discipline, but you have a chance to do a better job with the children you care for. If reflecting on your childhood brings back unresolved issues, seek help from a friend, a program director, or a counselor. You may use a variety of discipline approaches to try to avoid using the same approaches you experienced as a child. This avoidance may be because of negative feelings, bad memories, and/or guilt. Whatever the reason, you need to provide children with the necessary and appropriate discipline needed.

What was your experience with discipline as a child?

_____

_____

_____

How do you think this has affected your discipline style in the classroom?

_____

_____

_____

winning ways

Interactive Discipline and Direct Guidance

Can you see how these different disciplining styles can affect the behaviors happening in your classroom? Aim for a balanced, loving approach by using the interactive discipline style. It takes some practice, and one of the best methods for practicing an interactive discipline style is called *direct guidance*.

Direct guidance is a positive way to interact with children and guide them to success. Below are some effective direct guidance techniques. Review these tips and think about how you can adopt them to improve your interactions with young children. When you put them to use *before* your classroom is out of your control, you'll notice fewer behavioral concerns.

9 PRINCIPLES OF DIRECT GUIDANCE

- Use simple language.
- Speak in a relaxed voice.
- Offer choices carefully.
- Encourage independence and cooperation.
- Be firm.
- Be consistent.
- Provide time for change.
- Consider children's feelings.
- Intervene when necessary.

Manage Your Classroom

Classroom management is how you help the children in your classroom learn to regulate their own behavior in response to what's going on around them. What can you do to help children learn self-control? It's harder to stick with a diet if you have ice cream, cake, and cookies in your house. Classroom management includes how you set up your environment, your expectations, and your teaching style. Take a deep look at your own skills and ask yourself, *Can I improve my classroom management skills? Can we, as a team, do something better?* Routinely evaluating yourself can help you catch and prevent challenging behaviors more quickly and create a positive learning environment for all the children.

Assessing My Classroom Management

Are my expectations realistic for my age group?

Yes ☐   No ☐

Do I have a limited number of appropriate rules?

Yes ☐   No ☐

Are my lesson plans prepared?

Yes ☐   No ☐

Are supplies readily available?

Yes ☐   No ☐

Is there full teacher-child interaction with every child?

Yes ☐   No ☐

Are children's waiting times limited?

Yes ☐   No ☐

Describe your teaching style. Share your thoughts about aspects of your classroom management here:

_____

_____

_____

_____

_____

_____

_____

_____

_____

winning ways

Remember Your Environment

Classrooms often look the best in the morning before children arrive. Think about a store where you dig in bins for bargains. Now think about another store where every sweater is folded neatly. That's called *merchandising*. It's your responsibility to merchandise your room, to make it active, functional, engaging, and fun for young children. You don't need a degree in retail to try these ideas out and become a good early childhood professional.

* Is your space age appropriate?
* Is there enough space for physical movement?
* Is it warm and inviting?
* Is it organized, clean, and uncluttered?
* Are the manipulatives organized and labeled?
* Are children able to move freely without obstructions?

Review chapter 2 for more about the importance of creating a successful learning environment.

Set Realistic Expectations

Expectations are the infinite rules of life that children need to learn—what they should do or shouldn't do. These expectations can be pretty simple: "Please don't talk with your mouth full," or "Use a quiet voice in the class." Whatever your expectations, they need to be specific and attainable. If your expectations are unreasonable, children's behavior will reflect that. Never achieving goals is frustrating for anyone, children included.

Are your expectations easy to follow? Or are they almost impossible for young children? How long can *you* sit still and listen?

Here are some expectations I currently have for the children in my classroom:

_____

_____

_____

_____

Put a check beside the expectations that are realistic. Now circle the ones that may be too difficult for children.

guiding challenging behavior

Why Should Your Expectations Be Specific?

Children often don't understand what you want them to do or not do. You have to be really specific if you expect them to do as you say. When you say you want children to clean up after lunch, include *what* and *how* you would like them to clean up. Which version of this request do you think is more specific?

- Line up for outside.

- Please, line up quietly by the door, one behind the other, so we can go outside.

Not hard to guess, but much harder to do. Now take the following expectations and make them more specific.

- Clean up.

  _____

- Get ready for lunch.

  _____

Age-Appropriate Expectations

What are children capable of successfully doing at their age? Can a two-year-old share a toy without protest as an eight-year-old can? Sharing may be on your to-do list of expectations, but the ability to share may differ depending on the child's age. Teachers often expect children to do things they're not yet capable of. Sometimes children just need your help getting organized or breaking the task into smaller steps.

Let's look at an example. The children have been playing, and toys are everywhere. You say, "Please clean up the toys." Depending on the children's age and attention to detail, they may feel completely overwhelmed and not even know where to start. Some children may then avoid the task of cleaning up, which from your perspective, might look like not listening. Other children might put the toys in one big pile or shove them behind the shelves. In this case, the children need more specific direction and a lot of your help.

Assess Your Teaching Style

Every teacher has a slightly different teaching style. Are you a rule enforcer, or are you laid back, or do you just manage to get through the busy day? Consider your teaching style when you're making rules, redirecting children, and focusing your attention. Self-awareness will help you better understand how you personally affect behavior in the classroom.

Too Many Rules?

How can there ever be too many rules? There can be. Make sure your classroom rules are clear, specific, and appropriate—and then you'll need fewer of them.

CLASSROOM RULES

1 **Walk inside.**

2 **Listen to others.**

3 **Use a quiet voice.**

4 **Help clean up.**

5 **Use your words when you are upset.**

Guidelines for Making Classroom Rules

1 Have the children help make the rules if they are old enough.

2 List the rules in the positive form; for example, use "Walk" instead of "Don't run."

3 Write the rules on a large poster to refer back to, even if most children can't yet read, so everyone knows the rules.

4 Use photographs or pictures to illustrate the rules.

5 Have children sign the rules to show they agree. Some may just make a crayon mark or scribble.

6 Review the rules periodically.

7 Refer the children back to the rules when they break them.

8 Add a new rule if the children suggest it, but avoid too many rules.

guiding challenging behavior

17 Ways to Help Children Avoid Discipline Problems

Here's a quick list of tips and ideas to keep discipline problems at a minimum. You should refer to it throughout the day.

1 Develop a consistent routine to help children feel secure and teachers feel prepared.

2 Children understand the sequence of routines: *This comes first, then this comes next.*

3 Plan more active than quiet time for young children.

4 Cleanup and transition times often take longer than the activities themselves. That's okay. Relax and realize that these are learning times too. Make them fun times as well!

5 Long periods of waiting or quiet activities like coloring usually lead to acting-out behaviors, especially in more active children.

6 If your room seems chaotic, sing. Keep a list of songs at hand so that you are never at a loss.

7 Routine should provide a framework for class management, but allow for flexibility when children are really interested in a certain activity and need more time.

8 Have materials and curriculum completely prepared before starting your day so you can give children your full attention.

9 Resist chatting with other adults about personal matters while children are in your care.

10 Realize that teaching children positive behavior is more important than any other activity.

11 Remember that children require a great deal of reminding and reminding and reminding.

12 Model for the children the way you want them to speak: "May I please have the glue?"

13 Notice and acknowledge when children behave well. "I liked the way you asked for the paper." "You're really listening to the story. Thank you."

14 Guide children who are hesitant or indecisive and may need your help to choose activities, especially during free play.

15 Offer children choices only when choice is possible. If everyone is going outside, then staying inside may not be a choice. "We are going outside. Do you want to play on the swings or kick the ball?"

16 Try to offer only two choices when possible. Instead of "Where do you want to sit?" ask, "Would you like to sit here or here?" and point to the options.

17 Be flexible. A child may choose blue and then want green. Let him have the green. How many times have you changed your mind when ordering from a menu or picking out clothes? (Some of you may have more trouble with this than others.)

winning ways

It's easy to become overwhelmed and anxious when you work with young children, especially with those who exhibit challenging behaviors. Are you eagerly waiting for that perfect day, the day when all your children will sit quietly and listen to your every word? When you are working with young children, that perfect day never really comes. Instead, there are things you can do to support children's positive behaviors. Keeping realistic expectations and understanding your individual teaching style will help you succeed. Next, you'll explore how to observe the behavior of children. Observation will help you examine their behavior more closely so you can look for ways to help them.

OPTIMIZE YOUR KNOWLEDGE

1 Which type of discipline style do you relate to most? Explain why.

_____

_____

_____

2 Create a list of rules for your classroom.

_____

_____

_____

3 Why are realistic expectations important? List an expectation that you once had in the classroom that you now realize is unrealistic.

_____

_____

_____

guiding challenging behavior

4

Observe, Observe, Observe!

4

I regularly observe my classroom and each child to understand the behaviors in the classroom.

○ Always

○ Usually

○ Sometimes

○ Never

What Is an Observation?

An *observation* is really *seeing* what is going on in your classroom. When you want to know more about what's happening in your classroom or with a specific child, use observations. An observation allows you to take a peek in your classroom from a different angle—you often see behaviors and patterns you didn't notice when you were in the middle of the hustle and bustle of the day.

What an observation looks like depends on what we're observing for. Sometimes an observation looks like a teacher just separating herself from the room by sitting in a corner, recording notes. Or it might look like a teacher or an administrator watching the classroom from an outsider-looking-in perspective. You observe to collect information about children's preferences, fears, personality, achievements, developmental skills, and much more. No matter how you approach observations, your goal is to learn more about children or their environment.

Why Bother Observing?

What exactly are you looking for when you observe a classroom or a particular child? You might look for behaviors, reactions, developing skills, or a particular goal a child has achieved. It's likely that you'll also see things that surprise you, but you should still begin each observation with clear goals in mind.

Observation GOALS

- Learn about a child's individual likes and dislikes.
- Discover a child's behavioral patterns.
- Make note of a child's progress.
- Identify areas to adjust in your lesson planning.
- Collect anecdotes for parent/teacher conferences.
- Evaluate the environment.
- Reflect on your own teaching strategies.

What other goals might you have for observations?

- _____

- _____

Plan Observations Early and Often

If you want to understand what's happening in your classroom, you need to observe it regularly. During observations, focus your attention and record what's happening in the classroom at different times. When observing routinely, look at the overall classroom, what is working, what is not, whether certain children tend to play together, which children like to engage in solitary play. You get it. Routine observations can help you assess what you need to do differently to help prevent challenging behaviors.

Plan Routine Observations

We observe routinely in order to

❯ understand each child more deeply,

❯ track whether children are achieving their developmental goals,

❯ identify successful and challenging activities or times of day,

❯ discover environment concerns, and

❯ identify potential challenging behaviors.

guiding challenging behavior

Make It Happen: Schedule Your Observations

Set a time and stick to it. This is the first step to successful observation. Integrate regular observations into your schedule. They can be every Tuesday morning at 10:00 a.m., or they can be every time your floater overlaps for a half hour with a teacher who's leaving. Mix up the times to see different periods of the day.

Once you make time for these routine observations, they will become second nature. Many things need to happen throughout the day, such as changing, feeding, and engaging and interacting with the children. Think of observations as snapshot of your classroom. Once you take mental pictures of your room, you can pinpoint when the rhythm or patterns in your room change. However, if you don't have the picture from a month or a week ago, it's easy to miss those differences.

The Administrator's View of Your Classroom

Consider the dreaded monthly observation. You know, the one where an administrator comes into your classroom and the following happens:

- You freeze up, get red in the face, and start stuttering.

- The children start screaming, running around in circles, climbing walls, and jumping off chairs.

- One of your coworkers is nowhere to be found: he's in the bathroom, getting art supplies, or somewhere else (aka "hiding").

If that sounds like your experience, you're not alone! The thing is, observations aren't about looking for things that are going wrong. Instead, observations are an insight into your classroom. Ever say to yourself, *I wish there was a better way to do this*, or *I wish this transition could go a little smoother*? Well, have an outside observer visit your classroom, and you'll get a new perspective on things. Maybe your administrator will catch a behavior that you think is typical and ask you to keep an eye on it, or maybe she'll suggest a change in your environment or schedule that could improve transitions. Administrative observations are a look into the overall functioning of your classroom, but they can also help catch things that aren't quite right before an issue even starts.

Who Can Observe?

Observations aren't just for administrators. You could invite a range of people to observe your room. Every person who observes your room may notice different things, and that's a good thing!

Who Should Conduct an Observation in Your Classroom?

- *Lead teachers*
- *Float teachers*
- *Directors*
- *Assistant teachers*
- *Office staff*
- *Parents*

Phone a Friend

Any of your work colleagues can help conduct observations. Ask a coworker, a friend, or a mentor to come in and watch how you run your room. Or ask an assistant to switch classrooms or double up, as appropriate, making sure to keep ratio! A fresh set of eyes will be able to provide a lot of insight.

Are observations currently part of your responsibilities? If yes, explain how. If no, who conducts observations in your program?

_____

_____

_____

_____

_____

guiding challenging behavior

Whole Classroom Observations

Take a minute to think about your classroom as if you were on the outside looking in. In an ideal world, a routine observation would provide evidence that your classroom is flowing nicely, that it's safe, the children are engaged, all your transitions are smooth, and you can see that the children are all reaching their developmental milestones. Of course, that ideal world rarely happens—but a classroom observation allows you to see what's working and what's not. What you end up seeing and learning from these observations can help you tremendously. For instance, you might notice how the transition from lunch to nap isn't working. You may not see these small speed bumps because you live them every day, and sometimes frustration becomes the norm. Observing your own classroom will help you create a more successful environment and overall schedule.

What to Observe When You're Observing

With observation, the sky's the limit, but here are some common things to look for:

- Are the children happy and engaged?
- Are they meeting developmental goals?
- Are transitions smooth? How can they be improved?
- Are prime times such as diapering, feeding, and getting ready to go outside completed easily?
- Are there times of day that influence certain behaviors?
- Are there activities, such as naptime or lunch, that perpetuate certain behaviors?
- How do different teachers affect the classroom's routines and behaviors?
- Which centers or learning areas are popular?
- Which centers or learning areas can be improved?
- Does each child have a favorite peer or peer group?
- Where and when do conflicts happen?

Individual Child Observations

Doing an *individual child observation* means focusing on one particular child. When you observe individual children, you look for their strengths and weaknesses, behavior patterns, preferences, personality, and more. To collect this kind of information, you or an observer will stand unobtrusively in the classroom and record the child's activities without interrupting the child. When observing, you can also collect samples of the child's work, take assessments, or photograph the child in the midst of an activity. Once you've collected information from individual observations, you can better understand children's behaviors and create a more individualized learning program for each child. Individual observations can also document when challenging behaviors occur.

It may seem overwhelming to think about conducting individual observations on all the children in your classroom, given the many tasks you must complete throughout the day. And that's aside from the not-so-easy task of supervising and caring for fifteen-plus children! Just about everything you do in an early childhood classroom is only successful with a strong team. Observations are no different.

Plan, Plan, Plan!

Again, set aside some time for each teacher to observe the classroom at different times. You may be thinking, *There is no way I can spare a teacher's set of hands.* But you can, you can! It will benefit *all* of you in the end. Think of it like this: when you have challenging behaviors in your classroom, it seems you can never get enough help. If you complete the observations and catch behaviors before they hit that point, your days will be more about children learning and less about tackling children's challenging behaviors. Prioritizing time for classroom observations now will save you time in the future and help counteract or ease some of those challenging behaviors.

List some times you can make available for classroom observations.

_____

_____

Ready to give it a shot?

I pledge to give myself time to complete observations of my classroom to benefit us all.   INITIAL HERE: _____

guiding challenging behavior

Can You Be a Good Observer?

Observing becomes engaging once you are focused. You start to see things you never noticed before, and the reason for behavior becomes clearer. Use the following questions as guidelines to prepare for an observation.

How Are Your Observation Skills?

1	Can you give your undivided attention to an observation?	Always	Sometimes	Never
2	Can you be objective and free of assumptions?	Always	Sometimes	Never
3	Do you know what is developmentally appropriate?	Always	Sometimes	Never
4	Do you have a specific goal in mind?	Always	Sometimes	Never
5	Can you describe the environment?	Always	Sometimes	Never
6	Do you have a schedule for conducting observations?	Always	Sometimes	Never
7	Do you have a method of recording observations?	Always	Sometimes	Never

What do you think is the biggest challenge in being an observer?

_____

_____

_____

_____

_____

_____

_____

_____

winning ways

What do you need to do to overcome this challenge?

_____

_____

_____

_____

_____

_____

_____

Recording Your Observations

As a teacher in early child care, you sure have a busy day from start to finish! The easiest way to record your observations is to have a system. Observing will provide a lot of information. It is important to document everything you observe. Good observation documentation includes the following:

- The child's name
- Name of observer
- Specific date
- Begin time and end time
- Location: in classroom, on playground, etc.
- Descriptions of the behavior: actions, facial cues, verbal/social interactions
- Descriptive words, including lots of adjectives and adverbs

Because observations should happen more than once for each child, you may end up with plenty of notes! If a particular child continues to demonstrate inappropriate behavior, record the time and circumstances of each observation. By keeping track of this information through documentation, you may find a pattern of behavior. There may be certain times or situations when the child is more likely to act out. Use this information to anticipate and help the child avoid the behavior in the future.

DOCUMENTATION METHODS

You can use a range of documentation methods to keep track of your observations. Here are some ideas to try. See chapter 5 for some examples of forms.

Observation forms Forms that allow you to document any of your observations

Behavior documentation forms Forms that document observations of specific challenging behaviors

Checklists and assessments Forms that only require you to check off or fill in information on children's developmental goals

Record-keeping notebook A simple, small notebook

No one method is better than the others, and sometimes a mixture of methods can help you see all the angles of a situation. Feel free to experiment with different recording methods, and find the ones that are most helpful to you and your team.

Observation is an important component of any successful early childhood program, but many teachers don't make the time to observe. The more you practice observing, the more it becomes routine and second nature! Integrating regular observations into your daily classroom life will help you be prepared for specific challenging behaviors when they appear in your classroom. In chapter 5, we'll discuss observations as they relate to challenging behaviors.

OPTIMIZE YOUR KNOWLEDGE

1 Explain in your own words what observation is and why it is important in the early childhood classroom.

_____

_____

_____

_____

_____

2 List at least three reasons why you would plan routine observations.

_____

_____

_____

_____

3 Without naming names, describe a time when observing a child could have helped a situation in your classroom.

_____

_____

_____

_____

guiding challenging behavior

5

Observe and Understand Challenging Behaviors

When I have challenging behaviors in my classroom, I complete specific observations to better understand and help those children and situations.

- Always
- Usually
- Sometimes
- Never

How Routine Observations Help Challenging Behavior

In child care, observation is an ongoing process, not a one-time event. You should regularly observe your classroom and individual children regardless of whether you're experiencing behavior issues. When you regularly observe each child, you have a better sense of what behaviors are typical and what behaviors are unusual and challenging for that child. By conducting observations regularly, you can understand who children are, their strengths, challenges, and preferences—and you may be able to anticipate problems or issues before they begin. When you observe behavior that you know is problematic, you more clearly understand it and find ways to respond.

Focusing on Challenging Behavior

If—make that *when*—challenging behavior appears in your classroom, your observations should focus specifically on how you can help those children and improve those behaviors.

What to OBSERVE about Challenging Behavior

When you record your observations of challenging behavior, consider the following:

Certain times: Is group time too long for children to sit still? Is this the only time they display challenging behavior?

Nap: Do they refuse to sleep? Are they falling asleep at the lunch table?

Eating time: Do you notice the children displaying challenging behavior when they are last to sit for lunch?

Teacher switch: Have you noticed that all the reported accidents happen when Teacher A leaves for the day and Teacher B is left in charge?

Certain children: Does the challenging behavior happen when the same children play together?

Off routine: Do you notice a difference in behavior when children come into school later than usual or on Mondays?

Assess Children's Development

Challenging behavior can occur when children are not engaged at their own developmental level. If they exhibit challenging behavior and are not reaching appropriate developmental goals, that may be a sign that your expectations are too difficult for them or that they may meet milestones a little more slowly. In some cases, you may find that children have delays. That's when you ask for help. Every early childhood professional should know and understand the developmental milestones for each age group.

Practice Shadowing

Shadowing is another type of routine child observation that you can use to help with challenging behavior. Shadowing commits one teacher to the child displaying the inappropriate behaviors. When you're shadowing, you go everywhere the child goes. You become the child's "shadow" to try to understand what could potentially be affecting or causing the child's challenging behavior.

While shadowing, you need to follow the child's every move and document it all when possible. You should step in to prevent situations in which the child may self-harm or harm others, and you should direct the child from making poor choices. You should also record the child's attempts at challenging behavior, because documenting them can provide helpful information to determine any possible triggers or patterns of the reoccurring behavior.

Documenting Challenging Behaviors

When you conduct observations of challenging behavior or shadow a child, it is important to document your observations. Here is a documentation form that you can use to collect and organize your information.

DOCUMENTING BEHAVIORS

Use this form to document and review the incidents that occur with individual children, specific groups of children, and/or at specific times. Evaluate these observations to find patterns of behavior and to develop a plan to guide those behaviors differently.

Child's Name: _____

Child's Date of Birth: _____ Age: _____

Teacher's Names: _____

_____

Classroom: _____

	What I noticed: *behavior observed*	What else happened: *circumstances*	My reflections on what happened: *observations and possible causes*	My ideas to help the child or situation: *planning ahead*
DATE: TIME STARTED: TIME STOPPED:				
DATE: TIME STARTED: TIME STOPPED:				
DATE: TIME STARTED: TIME STOPPED:				
DATE: TIME STARTED: TIME STOPPED:				
DATE: TIME STARTED: TIME STOPPED:				
DATE: TIME STARTED: TIME STOPPED:				

winning ways

Tips for Successful Observations

Your observations will get better with practice and experience. Keep some best practices in mind to complete an accurate observation of challenging behavior. Here are some best practices:

Focus on . . . Observing

Observing with undivided attention may seem like a daunting task. The children will notice that you are not participating as usual. "Miss Gigi, what you are doing?" "I'm watching all the things that are happening in the room so I can make it an even more fun place to play and learn." Other teachers in the room can redirect the children if necessary.

Facts Are Facts

Being objective requires that you do not let personal feelings, opinions, or assumptions influence your observation. Observations require you to look for facts. You will find that it's easy to describe what *you thought you saw* or maybe even *what you want to see*.

Picture this: Dante is at the table with two other friends, and Miss Sara puts out a handful of Silly Putty in front of each of them. Dante stares at Miss Sara as she encourages him to touch the Silly Putty. He touches it once, then walks away. Miss Sara snaps a picture of Dante touching the Silly Putty and sends it to his parents with the caption, "Dante loved playing with the Silly Putty today!"

From the initial description, is this accurate? Is it a fact? These are the questions you should ask yourself when writing observations. Does Miss Sara know that Dante really loved the Silly Putty? How does she know that? Did he smile or laugh? Or did he keep the straight face Miss Sara assumed is his "I love this" face? The teacher's description is not factual. She made an assumption. But because she sent a picture *saying* Dante loved the Silly Putty, his parents are now confused about why Dante refuses to play with the Silly Putty they just bought him for home! Happens. All. The. Time.

Practice Being Objective

Try finding the objective observations in these descriptions:

1   James was playing in the block center. He picked up the colored blocks and placed them on top of each other. First he picked up the red, then the blue, then the red again, and then the blue. As the tower grew, he got up and continued placing the blocks on top of each other, red, blue, red, blue.

Is this description objective? What type of information does it give you regarding his learning abilities and/or behavior?

_____

_____

2 Sofia did not like playing dress-up. She thought there were too many kids in the center, so she got angry. Sofia threw all the baby dolls on the ground and threw a fit.

Is this description objective? What type of information does it give you regarding her learning abilities and/or behavior?

_____

_____

What did you notice about the first and second examples? The first description is much more objective: it gives facts and it is descriptive. James was in the block center using his fine-motor skills while exploring the blocks, and he can create patterns effectively.

The second description assumes that Sofia did not like the dress-up area and that she thought there were too many kids in the center. How did the observer know that? Did Sofia say that? The observer connected Sofia's anger to the assumption that Sofia thought the center was crowded without facts to back the assumption. The observer was accurate that Sofia threw all the dolls on the ground, but the observation is clouded by many inaccurate details based on assumptions about how Sofia feels. An objective observer should describe the actual events that happened as clearly as possible, leaving feelings out.

Being an objective observer is not an easy task! Remember to state what you *see*, not what you *think* you see. Ask yourself repeatedly, "Is this a fact?"

Know What You're Looking For

Observations are more useful if you know what you are looking for. You can refer to your curricular goals and observe to see if each child is achieving those goals. You can look specifically for social interaction.

When you are doing an individual observation focused on challenging behavior, make sure to focus on just the child's behavior. You want to make note of appropriate as well as inappropriate behavior. Make sure you are looking for the following:

- What happened right before the behavior
- What happened right after the behavior
- How children and teachers responded to the behavior

Keeping these questions in mind will help you to understand what might have made the child act a particular way and to possibly prevent the challenging behaviors.

The first step to successfully guiding challenging behavior in your classroom is to observe it. Solutions for these behaviors don't always come easily. This is where teamwork and action planning come in! In the next chapter, we'll look at creating action plans with your team. Team action planning is part of the process of helping each child succeed.

OPTIMIZE YOUR KNOWLEDGE

1   Observe one child in a classroom for at least ten minutes. Document what you see.

_____

_____

_____

2   How could shadowing a child be helpful to you?

_____

_____

_____

3   Why is being objective in observations and documentation important?

_____

_____

_____

guiding challenging behavior

6

Create an Action Plan as a Team

After observing challenging behavior in children, I work with my team to determine patterns and issues and create an action plan for those children.

- ○ Always
- ○ Usually
- ○ Sometimes
- ○ Never

Who's on Your Team?

You should review your observations to reflect on what you've learned about the children. When situations seem too complex for a quick classroom change, you need to create an action plan. It helps if you have the whole team on board. Keep in mind that some parents may be uncooperative when the school first shares behavioral concerns. Denial, reflection, or responses such as "It's the school's fault" are not unusual or abnormal. Even your program administrators may need a little persuasion to get them into the classroom. Be patient and persistent. And make sure you've included your entire team in this process.

Your team may include the following:

- Coworkers: any teachers who also work with or have worked with the child
- Administrators: director, assistant director, principal
- Caregivers: parents, guardians, other family members who are caregivers
- On-staff resources: social worker, family coordinator, education coordinator

Who else might be on your team? Can you think of others? List them here:

_____

_____

_____

You should discuss your observations with your director or supervisor on a regular basis. When you discuss your concerns, be honest and clear about your concerns. Asking for help to guide the challenging behavior of a child does not indicate that you are weak or incapable. Just the opposite: strong advocates for children ask for help.

Evaluate the information you collected and create an action plan to address concerns that are found through observations, whether you're addressing a single child's challenging behavior or multiple issues in your classroom environment.

Ready, Set, Reflect!

You've trailed the children around, taken careful notes of every incident or near-incident, and cleaned up a few spills in the process. Now what? Observing challenging behavior doesn't stop with recording your observations and shadowing. After you've taken the time to observe the challenging behavior, it's time to evaluate what you've learned and act on it. This isn't something you can do alone—just about everything in an early learning classroom requires teamwork, and analyzing observations successfully is no different!

What Do You Look for When You Reflect?

Take the time to review all of your notes so you understand the situation. Reflecting after observing helps you do the following:

- Identify children who need additional help
- Plan for individualized education and care
- Invite the resources of special early childhood services
- Evaluate the quality of the program
- Identify program needs
- Determine necessary staff training

Reflecting as a Team

What are the factors or possible reasons that certain behaviors, whether appropriate or inappropriate, may be happening? What insights can your observations give you? Review all of your notes and look for patterns. Consider questions like these:

- What happened right before the behavior occurred?
- What happened right after the behavior occurred?

guiding challenging behavior

- How did children and teachers respond to the behavior?
- Does time of day seem to affect certain behaviors or events?
- Are there activities (such as naptime or lunchtime) or routines that increase certain behaviors or events?
- How do different teachers affect the classroom's routines and behaviors?
- How strong are children's self-help skills?
- What centers or learning areas do children enjoy most?
- Do children have a favorite peer or peer group?
- Where do conflicts typically happen?
- What types of conflicts typically happen?

Repeated behavior typically has a trigger. Take your time to look for patterns and consider multiple angles. Once you identify possible triggers and problem areas, you can take steps to guide those behaviors and situations in a positive direction.

Let's Practice!

Look at the chart on the opposite page and review the incidents that are described. What patterns do you see? Can you find a common theme in the challenging behaviors? Remember to keep your report factual and objective.

Review this chart and pay attention to the details! See if you can pinpoint patterns or issues and write them below. If you have possible solutions, fill those in below as well!

▶ What patterns do you see? What specific issues do you notice?

_____

_____

_____

▶ What possible solutions or steps could these teachers take to prevent these behaviors?

_____

_____

_____

winning ways

TRACKING BEHAVIORS

Child's Name: _____

Child's Date of Birth: _____ Age: _3 yrs. old_

Teacher's Names: ___Ms. Jen, Ms. Mary___

Classroom: ___Tigers___

	What I noticed: behavior observed	What else happened: circumstances	My reflections on what happened: observations and possible causes	My ideas to help the child or situation: planning ahead
DATE: 5/15 TIME STARTED: 9:25 TIME STOPPED: 9:37	Jack hit John over the head with blocks	5 children in block center, one teacher in room		
DATE: 5/16 TIME STARTED: 10:00 TIME STOPPED: 10:16	In the block center, Samantha bit Alex	6 other children in block center, crowded		
DATE: 5/17 TIME STARTED: 9:42 TIME STOPPED: 9:53	Tim threw himself on the floor, kicking and screaming, after playing tug-of-war with Sammy over the big construction blocks	Blocks were being cleaned, only one bin of blocks		

Here's What We Noticed

In this example, a common factor in each situation is where the behavior took place: in the block center. Miss Jen and Miss Mary need to pay special attention to the block center. They may need to provide a larger space, add more manipulatives, or reorganize it.

The block center incident is a simple, straightforward example, but you'll be surprised how many of these situations have an equally simple fix if you document and analyze them. It's amazing how often a difficult situation has a simple cause and a reasonable solution.

"I thought that's what I'm supposed to do":
Thoughts from Jeniece

When you're observing, another way to figure out or identify patterns is by simply asking, "What is wrong? What is bothering you?" For those children who are vocal enough, it may be as simple as that.

I'll never forget the first time I realized that sometimes you just have to ask a child a question. Natalie was two going on three years and new to the school. She cried during every drop-off. She was very intelligent, vocal, and kind—when she stopped crying. Her mom was concerned—as much as I kept saying Natalie needed an adjustment period and that it would soon pass, these reassurances just didn't sit right with Natalie's mom.

We were a few weeks into school, and Natalie still wouldn't stop crying at drop-off. It wasn't a few tears, either; it was a full-blown "Mommy, don't leave me here" cry. Soon after her concerned mom left, she would calm down. "We promise she's fine after you walk out the door!" we would say. Natalie was fine in the classroom, so we assumed her crying was a result of something at home or something that happened before drop-off. What happened right before drop-off? Did her routine change?

Finally, one morning, Natalie's mom came in smiling ear to ear and proudly handed Natalie over to me. She said, "Natalie, tell Ms. J. why I'm so happy." Natalie replied, "Because I will not cry today!" I stood there, mouth open, while Natalie's mom told me that last night before bedtime, she had finally asked the question: "Natalie, why do you cry each time I leave you at school? Don't you like it? Don't you like Ms. J.?" Natalie had said, "I thought that's what I'm supposed to do. We cry when we go to school, then we play!"

Natalie had originally been crying because of the adjustment, and when everything else became so routine for her, it seemed like crying was supposed to start off her day. It probably didn't help that other children sometimes cried at drop-off. Children often copy one another. Natalie never cried again at drop-off. We may not always have a child reply so matter-of-factly, and children are not always this communicative, but it doesn't hurt to try!

Create an Action Plan

After you have observed, recorded, and evaluated behaviors or behavioral patterns, it is time to make an action plan. What is an action plan? It is your plan to help children improve their behavior. Your action plan includes the following:

- The problem
- Possible causes of the problem
- Possible solutions to the problem
- The person responsible for carrying out the solution(s)

Action plans typically involve collaborators because it is rare for a teacher to be the only one in the classroom; you need a team!

Set aside time to create an action plan if you have challenging behavior in your classroom. Work with a coteacher, an administrator, or even a parent. Typically, a teacher and administrator work together to create the plan and implement it. It is up to you and your administrator whether you want to include and let the parent know what you are working on. If you are going to share your observation and action plan with a parent, include the parent from the beginning.

What Do We Do Now?

To create an action plan, you must clearly identify (a) the current behaviors you want to change, and (b) what you want those behaviors to become instead. Think of these two things as "point A" and "point B." Then you need to decide how to get from point A to point B. You also have to keep in mind:

- How quickly you put the plan in place
- Who is going to participate or collaborate with the plan

Include all of the teachers you work with in your classroom. For the plan to work, you need to be consistently carrying out your action plan to achieve the desired behavior. Consistency is key. If your lead teacher for the action plan is absent one day, you need to be confident that the other teachers can implement it in her absence. Inconsistency in guiding challenging behavior may lead to even more challenging behavior.

YOUR ACTION PLAN

With your team, record any behavioral issues in your classroom and identify your next steps for actions to improve these behaviors.

BEHAVIORAL ISSUE OR CHALLENGING BEHAVIOR	POSSIBLE ENVIRONMENTAL CAUSES	DESIRED BEHAVIOR	STEPS TO ACHIEVE DESIRED BEHAVIOR	OBSERVING TEACHER & COLLABORATORS

winning ways

From *Guiding Challenging Behavior* by Gigi Schweikert, Jeniece Decker, and Jennifer Romanoff, © 2016. Published by Redleaf Press, www.redleafpress.org. This page may be reproduced for program use only.

What Do Action Plans Look Like?

Here are some examples of what action plans look like. In the first one, a teacher has noticed that the children are constantly running around. She takes the time to observe her classroom and puts together an action plan based on her observation.

BEHAVIORAL ISSUE OR CHALLENGING BEHAVIOR	POSSIBLE ENVIRONMENTAL CAUSES	DESIRED BEHAVIOR	STEPS TO ACHIEVE DESIRED BEHAVIOR	OBSERVING TEACHER & COLLABORATORS
Running around the classroom	Wide running spaces, shelves against wall	Children engaged in small groups at desired center areas	Set up classroom into small learning centers, satellite furniture to divide up runways	Miss J.
Difficulty moving to playground	Walkway is narrow and one class has to leave the playground at the same time we are entering it	Children walking to playground from classroom in a quiet and orderly fashion	Coordinate with teacher of other class. Both of us line up our classes and sing a transition song while doing so	Miss J. and Miss P.

Next is an example of an action plan for an individual child. If a specific child is having repeated challenging behavior, you can create an action plan that looks something like this.

BEHAVIORAL ISSUE OR CHALLENGING BEHAVIOR	POSSIBLE ENVIRONMENTAL CAUSES	DESIRED BEHAVIOR	STEPS TO ACHIEVE DESIRED BEHAVIOR	OBSERVING TEACHER & COLLABORATORS
Pushing at circle time	Too many unengaged children on the carpet	No pushing, children keep their hands to themselves	Switch up circle time to be engaging and exciting. Prepare for an extra teacher to be interacting with children at circle time	Miss J., ask Miss M. to sit at circle time instead of prepping bulletin board
Hits same child at lunch table	Does not enjoy the company of child he is sitting next to	Keeping hands to self	Discuss with child, switch seating arrangement	Miss J. and Miss M.

guiding challenging behavior

Finally, here is an example of an action plan with an emphasis on showing how to involve the parents doing the same thing at home to help reinforce the desired behaviors.

BEHAVIORAL ISSUE OR CHALLENGING BEHAVIOR	POSSIBLE ENVIRONMENTAL CAUSES	DESIRED BEHAVIOR	STEPS TO ACHIEVE DESIRED BEHAVIOR	OBSERVING TEACHER & COLLABORATORS
Child biting	Not working in small group interactions	Parallel or cooperative play without conflict, injury, or unacceptable behaviors	Work in small groups of children throughout the day so that the biting child is "shadowed" by a staff member in each group he/she participates in.	Miss J. to use minimal language with the biter—focusing mainly on bitten child. Meeting with parents to discuss collaborative effort in reinforcement of acceptable behavior in the home.
Temper tantrums	Moving children from one learning center to another	Engaged children in small group learning centers	Let children choose the center in which they would like to play. If tantrums occur, supervise them from a distance while continuing to interact with all other children. When child is ready and sees there is not attention being given to the undesired behavior, the tantrums will begin to subside.	Miss J. will work with classroom teachers to ensure child is safe from surrounding items if tantrum should occur. Meeting with parents to discuss philosophy of dealing with tantrum to ensure a strong home-school connection to help child cease behavior.

You can say you observe your classroom all the time, but if you don't take the time to review the information, you'll have a hard time finding solutions to challenging behaviors. Relying on your team can help you begin to solve problems or situations that you may need to later discuss with parents. In the next chapter, we'll explore how to share information about challenging behavior with parents.

OPTIMIZE YOUR KNOWLEDGE

1   List your coworkers and their titles.

_____

_____

_____

_____

_____

2   Why is descriptive and accurate information so important in documentation?

_____

_____

_____

_____

_____

3   Explain the importance of an action plan and why it may help a child's challenging behavior improve.

_____

_____

_____

_____

_____

guiding challenging behavior

7

Manage Difficult Conversations with Parents

I prepare for and carefully handle difficult conversations with parents about their children's challenging behaviors.

- Always

- Usually

- Sometimes

- Never

Build Strong Parent Relationships

What do parent relationships and challenging behavior have to do with one another? Are you thinking, *Challenging behavior comes from the home?* Children can be shaped by their experiences at home, but typically developing children can learn to behave appropriately at school even if that's not what they are doing at home and even if the parents and school aren't on the same disciplinary page. Building a strong parent relationship is good for the care and education of all children. Read the Winning Ways book *Partnering with Families* for further information.

If you build strong relationships with parents when concerns such as challenging behavior arise, the parents may be more open to and cooperative with your observations and action plan to guide the child to success. Keep in mind that even in the best parent-teacher partnerships, when you tell parents that their child is acting out or that you have concerns, you may be met with anger, denial, frustration, or rationalization. But never give up. Relationships are important all of the time, but you will become uniquely reliant on them when challenging behavior occurs.

When to Involve Parents

You should be communicating daily with parents about their children's behavior. Let's say you've been on top of your daily communication with them, you have completed your observations, assessments, and action plans, and you've discussed all of the above with your administrators. Once you've taken all the necessary steps and you feel as if you still don't have a grip on children's challenging behavior, then it's time for a conversation with their parents. If you believe that children may require a specific care or educational strategy that is beyond your expertise, work with your director to share your concerns with the parents. Before communicating sensitive and potentially relationship-compromising information, you need to be confident that your concerns are valid. Relaying information to parents about challenging behaviors is a sensitive topic. When you have already built a relationship with each parent, you can decide the best way to approach each situation. If a child is biting or hitting in your classroom multiple times a day, putting other children in harm's way, or exhibiting other concerning behaviors, it is important to involve parents immediately while you continue to observe, document, and create action plans.

When Should You Have a Concerned Conversation with Parents?

Below are some questions for you to think about before speaking with parents or asking to schedule a meeting. It's best to prepare answers to some of the pertinent questions because parents may come ready to ask you a multitude of questions.

- Do you have a concern that the child may have a condition that is atypical?

- Do you think the child may benefit from early recognition and intervention?

- What behavior or absence of behavior concerns you? Describe it in detail.

There is no right, wrong, or direct answer to questions. However, if you notice your answers to most questions are somewhat serious and your gut is telling you something is "not right," be an advocate for the child and speak with the parents. Even if you are wrong, it's better to have a conversation and bring in additional resources than to be right and say nothing at all. That's why they're called difficult conversations.

Next, undertake the following steps:

- Document your concerns. Describe the behavior. Indicate the situation(s) in which it happens. Note the dates and times.

- Compare the child's behavior or absence of behavior to developmental norms.

- Bring the concern to the attention of your supervisor.

guiding challenging behavior

- Respect the child and family by maintaining confidentiality and limiting conversations with other staff members unless it concerns them.

- Share your concerns with the parents and be prepared for an emotional response, denial, or deflection of the issue back on you or the program.

- Develop a plan for further observation.

- Direct the parents to outside resources for consultation or get written permission from the parents to contact resources yourself.

- Learn how to better assist the child in your environment.

- Celebrate the successes and abilities of the child.

Have you ever spoken to parents about a child's challenging behavior? If so, describe what happened. If not, what would you say?

_____

_____

_____

Parent Meetings: Who's Invited?

Now you've come to the decision to schedule a parent meeting. Who you invite to the meeting will depend on the situation. You and your team or administrator may need to sit down and discuss the best route for a conversation with the family. You want the right people to be at the meeting, but you don't want to overwhelm them either. Starting with the director, teacher, and parents is usually the best first step. You may also include the following:

✳ Child's teacher(s)

✳ Administrator

✳ On-site resources, nurse, education coordinator

As a teacher, you usually have the most information. You are the one on the front line and can probably explain the situation with the most ease and comfort. In difficult conversations, it is always best that you have at least one other person from the program present at the parent meeting. This person, preferably the director, can bring more credibility and authority to the conversation. This person is an additional advocate for the child to help the parents recognize that the school's teachers and leadership are on the same page. The director can also provide witness to the conversation if the parents blame the teacher or the school.

Be Prepared

Think through how best to communicate. Sometimes it's hard to see eye to eye with parents because they are thinking, *They have no idea what I go through day to day.* As a teacher, you are probably thinking the same thing too. Don't get into an "us" versus "them" mentality. The only side you should ever take is that of the child. Families and programs should work together when possible.

When you speak to parents about their children, it's important to be sensitive to everyone involved. To prepare for a formal conversation, consider the situation from the parents' perspective. Ask yourself questions like these:

- Are they aware of classroom behavior expectations?

- Do they know what developmental norms are for the age of their child?

- Have I discussed any of my concerns with them before? I should have!

- How do I anticipate this parent will respond to the conversation?

The relationships you have built with parents could not be more important than at times like this. If you have good relationships with parents, they are more likely to trust you and know you are doing all you can to help.

When you speak with parents, be careful to consider their perspectives and honestly share your observations.

1 Make sure that you are objective when discussing your concerns. Do not express your frustration with their child or the situation.

2 Be positive and talk about the child's strengths and positive qualities.

3 Ask to speak to the parents in private or make plans for a telephone call. These are not the type of conversations to have around children or other parents.

4 Be clear and offer specific examples of what you see the child doing or not doing.

5 Be honest and direct about your concerns or questions.

6 Be compassionate and recognize the parents' sensitivities.

7 Do not judge the child or the parents.

8 Listen to the parents and try to understand their perspective.

9 Expect parents to respond in varying ways: anger, denial, tears.

10 Don't take the situation personally—remember, you are trying to help the child and the parents.

11 Apologize if you make a mistake or say something incorrectly.

guiding challenging behavior

Imagine Yourself Talking to a Parent

Do not name names, but think of a parent with whom you would avoid having a difficult conversation.

- Why would you want to avoid the conversation?
- How do you think this conversation would go and why?

_____

_____

_____

_____

_____

Consider some of these conversation starters when what you'll say is difficult:

➤ Thank you for meeting with us. We're eager to work together so that we can help your child be even more successful.

➤ We appreciate your cooperation by coming in.

➤ We care so much about your child and your family, and we want to bring some of our observations to your attention.

When to Communicate to All Parents

When you have typical challenging behavior, for example, biting, it's a good idea to address all the parents in the classroom. If there are a few children biting in the toddler room, the parents of the children being bitten are likely to ask, "What are you doing about it?" Remember confidentiality. You never give the names of the children who are biting, even when the parents ask. Work with your administrator on how to inform parents about challenging behaviors in the classroom. See the Winning Ways: *Guiding Challenging Behavior* page on the Redleaf Press website (www.redleafpress.org) for an example of ways to inform parents about challenging behaviors.

☆ *Believe in Yourself* ∾

You Are a Professional!

Professionals in the early childhood field often feel nervous about talking to parents about their child's challenging behavior. That's natural. In all situations in which you must deliver difficult messages to parents, ask yourself this simple question:

Am I doing the right thing for the child?

If the answer is yes, be persistent, even if it's hard. You are helping the child. You are passionate about your work, and it doesn't mean you know all the answers, but it does mean you will do all you can for the well-being of the children. Keep your advocacy in mind to boost your confidence.

Remember that you're a professional! You've taken the appropriate steps to discuss concerns with your administrator, and now you're ready to talk with parents. Always be confident in yourself and your work!

Sharing a Child's Behavior with Parents

Calling for a meeting sends up a red flag to parents. Most of them will panic and begin to think the worst. When you schedule a meeting, make sure you explain briefly what you will be discussing. "Could you meet with the director and me to discuss our observations in the classroom about [*child's name*] hitting other children more often, and the teacher as well? I know you're concerned, so let's meet as soon as possible to work together to help [*child's name*]." Assure them that you are looking forward to meeting and having uninterrupted time with them to discuss their child's progress. Just as you were objective and factual when you documented challenging behaviors, so you'll now need to present your information to parents in exactly the same way. Make your documentation available for parents to see. Your documentation can include the following:

- Appropriate developmental goals for the child's age group
- Classroom expectations
- Strengths of the child
- Areas of opportunity for growth for the child
- Past family conference forms
- Behavioral documentation forms
- Action plans
- Any other notes

Typical Parent Reactions

Parents will all react differently to your concerns, both during and after your meeting. You can't be prepared for every possible reaction, but here are a few typical ones.

- Anger

- "How could you accuse my child of having challenging behavior?"

- Denial/frustration

- "I've never seen her do that!"

- Sadness

- "I've noticed, but I didn't know what to do."

- Laughter (denial)

- "He'll grow out of this."

- Discomfort and uncertainty

- "Is it something I'm doing wrong? What happens now?"

- Fear

- "Is something wrong with my child? Do I have to find a new school?"

- Understanding

- "What's the plan? What are our next steps?"

winning ways

How Will You Respond?

How would you address each of these emotions and reactions?

Anger

"I realize you're angry. Anger is a normal response when parents who care are trying to be protective of their child."

Denial/frustration

"Children often act differently at school than at home. There are more children to interact with at school, and the expectations are different."

Sadness

"Most parents are not sure what to do when they see their child exhibiting this type of behavior. You're a caring parent, and we are here to work together to help your child and you."

Laughter (denial)

"Children grow out of many behaviors. That's what development is all about. But based on our experience, we want to help your child change that behavior now and not take the chance that he might not grow out of it."

Discomfort and uncertainty

"We don't think it's something you are doing wrong, but how we behave as adults toward the child can help or hinder the child's ability to behave appropriately. Let's work together to figure that out."

Fear

"We appreciate your concerns, and at this time we are going to work together to see if this program can meet the needs of your child."

Understanding

Write how you would respond to a parent's understanding reaction.

_____

_____

During meetings with parents, the best-case scenario is the parent who understands. Most parents aren't going to respond like that. In all situations, tell the parents that you are there to support them. Keep a commitment to honest discussion and problem solving to ensure that parent meetings are positive. In these meetings, everyone is going to have valid concerns and questions. Create a "We are all in this together" environment.

More Than Challenging Behavior

The possibility that something may be seriously wrong with their child will be an emotional earthquake for many parents. It will strike at the heart of their being, their present, future, and even their past as parents. Validate their feelings: "I know it is difficult to hear information like this about [*child's name*]." Let parents know you're there to help. "We're going to work through this challenging behavior together." Let parents know that you have taken the proper steps to support their child in your classroom. "Here's what we have tried so far. Do you have any ideas?"

Communication is vital to forging and maintaining strong parent relationships. As hard as these conversations may be for you and parents, it's always most important to be open and honest. Many times it's not just the information you give, but how you give it, that really matters. Make sure you have all of your information and documentation ready and available for the parents to see. Chapter 8 gives you some tips on contacting outside help and engaging additional resources for children who may have more than just challenging behavior.

OPTIMIZE YOUR KNOWLEDGE

1   Think about the parent you have the strongest relationship with. How would you approach a conversation about challenging behavior with this parent?

_____

_____

_____

_____

2   Name at least three ways to prepare for a conversation about a child's behavioral concerns with parents.

_____

_____

_____

_____

3   List at least three of the typical responses parents might have to a conversation about the behavior of their child and how you would respond.

_____

_____

_____

_____

guiding challenging behavior

8

Identify Additional Child Services

I support parents with additional services and resources to help children with behavioral challenges.

○ Always

○ Usually

○ Sometimes

○ Never

Leading Children to Success

When you're concerned about children's challenging behavior, you have learned several steps you can take to understand and guide their self-control and development. You should do the following:

- Observe the child's behavior carefully.
- Collect and record your observations.
- Analyze your information.
- Inform your administrator about your concerns.
- Create an action plan with your team.
- Speak with the child's parents about your concerns.

But what happens when you take all of these steps and the behaviors or situations do not improve? Sometimes children need more help than you are qualified to give. When thinking about a particular child, do you often wish, *If only I had more teachers in here, I could give this child one-on-one time all day*? In typical group settings, one-on-one attention happens briefly. If you're thinking this way often, it sounds as if it's time to be resourceful and reach out to more qualified people.

An IMPORTANT Note

As a teacher, you should learn more about certain behaviors, have another person observe your classroom and make recommendations, and make changes to your room and routine to set children up for behavioral success. You may *not* have a person from outside of your program, even from your public school system, observe a particular child without written permission from the parents. Wanting to help is a good thing, but the parents must cooperate and give permission if you want to bring in additional support for a particular child. If parents refuse to partner with additional resources under your guidance, you may find that you are no longer able to serve this family and the child. The director of the program, along with the board of directors of the school or any other governing agent, will make this final decision.

How Do You Know?

It may be difficult to come to the realization that a child is not successful in your environment. As you're deciding how to address challenging behavior, take note of whether your efforts to observe, assess, and redirect have affected the child's behavior in a positive way. If the behavior has escalated or remained the same, it may be time to call for additional help. For example, children over the age of three years who have frequent temper tantrums may have other issues that are causing their crying and aggressive outbursts, such as language and/or speech problems, medical problems, or stress related to home or school. If you feel that your responses to challenging behavior are not enough to help the child, speak with your supervisor to discuss meeting with the child's parents on a regular basis to locate additional diagnosis and treatment resources. In these meetings, you can provide resources to parents and encourage them to seek the help of other professionals.

Supporting Parents

When you tell parents that you've done everything you can to help their child's challenging behavior and then suggest additional resources, parents may think the worst. Make sure that they know you can bring resources into the child's classroom—you're not necessarily asking the family to leave your program! Emphasize and stress that you want to work *with* them, not *against* them.

guiding challenging behavior

When talking to parents about helping their child with additional resources, remember the following:

- Have a prepared list of additional resources to give to the parents.
- Prepare a letter on behalf of the parents for them to sign and send to their local public school for assessment and assistance.
- Know that your conversation does not need to be scripted or perfect.
- Let your interaction be real yet direct.
- Avoid judgmental or accusatory statements.
- Remain hopeful.

It may take parents several times of hearing your request before they agree. If the child is not hurting himself or others and the behavior is not too disruptive to the other children and staff, give the parents time to comprehend and act on your offered assistance.

Know Your Limits

Providing care to parents does not mean that you are a social worker or counselor or that parents should expect such expertise from you. You can point families toward other resources that can help their children find additional services. It's important to know when to ask for an expert's input and when to hand over the situation to someone else.

Community Resources

As an early childhood professional, you should have a thorough knowledge of the resources available in your community. Once you know what's available, you can provide parents with pamphlets and phone numbers or offer to reach out on their behalf with their written permission. Common outside resources include the following:

- Child's pediatrician
- Early intervention services, if the child is under three years
- Child study team in public school, if child is over the age of three
- Private child psychologists
- Community programs
- Hotlines
- Local parents' groups

winning ways

What other resources could you use in your community?

★ _____

★ _____

★ _____

Let's look at three of the most accessible and frequently referred resources for parents: pediatricians, early intervention services, and child study teams.

Referring to a Child's Pediatrician

Pediatricians and other doctors are trained professionals who can help guide parents in the right direction. This is the first referral you should make. Parents often have a great deal of trust in their pediatricians. When you refer parents to their pediatrician, send them prepared. Write a condensed version of your observations, action plans, and findings. At the very least, copy all of your documentation for parents to take with them. Make sure the information you provide is clear, concise, and factual so that the pediatrician can work with all of the available information.

Referring to Early Intervention

The time between birth and three years is when most developmental delays are identified. As a teacher in an early childhood program, you have a unique opportunity to observe and watch children as they develop and learn. Early intervention helps parents of children under three years with assessment and services that are typically free of charge, regardless of parent income. The early intervention team is usually composed of a psychologist, a social worker, a learning consultant, an occupational therapist, a physical therapist, and a speech/language therapist. Contact your state licensing agency for resources in your community.

Referring to a Child Study Team

A child study team is usually a multidisciplinary group of professionals employed by the board of education to provide parents and teachers with a variety of learning-related services. As with early intervention teams, child study teams typically consist of a psychologist, a social worker, a learning consultant, an occupational therapist, a physical therapist, and a speech/ language therapist. These teams meet together and discuss what they can do to help. When you work with a child study team or refer parents to them, be prepared with clear documentation of your concerns, factual observations, and the plans you've tried so far. You're all on the same team, so any information you provide is a step forward.

guiding challenging behavior

Inviting Special Services to Your School

When parents start to work with experts and community resources, it may affect you and your classroom. Usually specialists and therapists want to see children in their most common or comfortable environments. Often that environment is your classroom. Working out these observations or interventions will require your collaboration, patience, understanding, and time. Remember, you are the one who led parents to the services in the first place.

Some special visitors may include the following:

- Applied behavior analysis (ABA) therapist
- Physical therapist
- Speech/language therapist
- Occupational therapist
- Any member of the child study team

Special services professionals may request to either visit your room or observe from outside of the classroom. Whichever they choose, remember that they are there to help the child. These professionals are not there to judge you, your program, or your environment. Below are some guidelines to review before they visit your classroom.

GUIDELINES FOR SPECIAL VISITORS

1 Know the person, date, time, and length of the session.

2 Alert the special services professional beforehand if the child is absent.

3 Have a predetermined place the professional will work with the child, such as in the classroom, an office, or a multipurpose room.

4 Ensure they have proper identification and credentials when they arrive.

5 Have a consistent schedule.

6 Introduce them to all of the children.

7 Answer questions when prompted about the child's daily activities.

8 Ask for advice on how to better respond to the child in your classroom.

winning ways

Keep Your Resources at Hand

Keep a list of outside resources and contact information available in your classroom or administrator's office. You may even want to add this information to your parent handbook and refer parents back to it. You can use a form like the one on page 80 or create your own. Here's an example—find out what groups and resources are available in your area.

ISSUE CONCERN	RESOURCE	CONTACT INFORMATION
Example: Autism	Autism Speaks	www.autismspeaks.org
Example: Speech delay, stuttering, lack of speech	Speech Delay	www.speechdelay.com

Accepting Reality

There's a saying that goes "You can lead a horse to water, but you can't make it drink." If you are reading through these chapters and thinking, *Did that. Done that. Yup, tried that. Ha! First thing I did . . .* then it might be time to accept reality: You as an early childhood educator may have done all you can to help this child with challenging behavior. There are two situations in which you may need to admit that as an early childhood educator, you have done all you can do.

1 You and your program are not properly qualified or equipped to care for the child.

2 A child's parents are not cooperative or willing to work with you to improve the situation.

Chapter 9 can help guide you to find the right place for a child in these situations.

guiding challenging behavior

RESOURCES FOR ADDITIONAL EARLY CHILDHOOD SERVICES

Our program is always looking for resources that can help us support you and your child. Here are some resources and groups we recommend. Feel free to ask us for more ideas!

ISSUE CONCERN	RESOURCE	CONTACT INFORMATION

winning ways

Being told that your child's challenging behavior may be something more than just typical inappropriate behavior can be scary and intimidating for most parents. Be prepared to help those families get the help they need. Knowing they have your support, not your judgment, can make all the difference in what may be a very difficult time for them. In the next chapter, we'll talk about the most difficult decision you and your program may ever make: deciding if you can serve and educate that child in the way he or she needs.

OPTIMIZE YOUR KNOWLEDGE

1 Why do early childhood educators sometimes refer parents to additional services?

_____

_____

_____

2 Research and list three specific community resources available in your area.

_____

_____

_____

3 Write about a time parents were uncooperative with their child's challenging behavior. Is there anything you could have done differently?

_____

_____

_____

guiding challenging behavior

9

Find the Place Where the Child Can Be Most Successful

I know my limits as an early childhood professional, and I support parents and children in finding the best place to ensure their success.

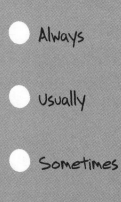

○ Always

○ Usually

○ Sometimes

○ Never

When It's Not the Right Fit

Teachers in many programs may encounter young children with special needs beyond the range of what is developmentally typical for their age: children with physical, emotional, cognitive, or family needs that require even more individualized attention. Occasionally you may be one of the first adults to recognize and suggest that your program may not be equipped with the resources to help a child be successful. If you then seek additional services for the child and see no improvement in the child's classroom life, you may have to ask the parents to remove their child from your program. When that happens, your role is to help find a place where the child can succeed.

Honesty Is the Best Policy

This may be the hardest chapter for us to write and for you to read, because asking a family to leave is one of the hardest things to do. If you must ask for a child to leave, you may feel as if you have failed. It is hard to accept that you've run out of options and that for the child's best interests, you need to send that family elsewhere. Instead of feeling as if you are "kicking the family out," think instead about "kicking the family in"—into where they need to be and where they can get the help and support they need.

When It's Time

When do you decide that you can no longer serve a child? It is always a painful experience for parents, staff, and the child. You should only ask a family to withdraw their child when your program has done everything it could to adapt to and support the child's needs. In cases where your program cannot serve certain children, you can work with parents to make a mutual decision that is peaceful and collaborative.

Sometimes you may ask a child to leave for one of two reasons involving challenging behavior:

1 You and your program are not properly qualified or equipped to educate or care for the child.

2 The parents are not cooperative or willing to work with you to improve the situation and to help the child.

How does this make you feel?

_____

_____

_____

Recognize, Appreciate, Address

Recognizing, appreciating, and addressing your differences is essential in early childhood education. Children may have special needs that change as they participate in your program. Whether their special needs are the result of sleepless nights, illness, separation problems, growth spurts, injuries, culture shock, or individual differences in temperament and physiology, the result is the same: *the program needs to fit the child,* not the reverse.

When you're working with challenging behavior, remember what your program provides and what your goals are. Children learn something in every setting. In this book, challenging behavior is defined as inappropriate behaviors that children exhibit consistently and that often require additional attention beyond what typical behavior requires. Challenging behavior can potentially harm adults, other children, or the children themselves. If children are still displaying challenging behavior after you have taken all appropriate steps outlined in this workbook, it's time to discuss with parents the possibility that your program may not be the right fit for their family.

guiding challenging behavior

Don't You Care? Of Course We Do

Though all children have special needs, many programs have young children whose conditions require consideration beyond that required for most children: developmental delays, disabilities, chronic illnesses, or family situations that put them at some risk. Providing good care and education to children with special needs is not the same as providing therapeutic or remedial services. The goals are the same as for any other children: high-quality care and education that fit each child's individual needs. While some programs may be able to provide specialists who offer special therapeutic or developmental services, all programs should partner with parents to identify resources that provide children with access to services beyond what your early childhood program offers.

The Americans with Disabilities Act (ADA) entitles people with disabilities to equal access to public services and public accommodations. Working parents of children with disabilities have the same need for child care that other parents do. Under ADA, programs have the responsibility to make reasonable accommodations to serve children and parents with disabilities. What is reasonable is in part determined by program resources, but programs may have to provide extra training, make changes to the facility, or alter program operations, including adjusting staff-child ratios.

Your Accommodations

Does your school currently enroll children with special needs?

Yes ☐   No ☐

If yes, what special accommodations does your school make?

_____

_____

_____

_____

Limitations

Every program has its limitations. You need to make sure that all the families in your program are aware of your goals, expectations, and standards. Some families might expect you to add more staff or not enroll as many children to achieve smaller group size, but that's not realistic for most programs. As a teacher, you need to communicate this important message to the families in your program: Our program will do the best we can to help and support you and your child within the expertise we provide.

"Us" versus "Them"

All parents want what is best for their children. When you must discuss a child leaving a school, it's easy for parents or staff to point fingers and blame others. Do not make this an "us" versus "them" situation. Be on the children's side. Parents have some of the same basic goals that you have for their children. For the most part, parents are working hard to do what's right for their children. Most parents want the following:

- What is best for their children
- To protect and provide for their children
- To give their children an education
- To make their children successful in school and life
- To have people like their children and to think they are good parents
- To give their children self-respect and self-esteem
- To keep their children physically healthy
- To help their children have friends

Can you think of a few other goals you and parents have in common?

_____

_____

_____

_____

_____

guiding challenging behavior

After a Family Has Left

Just because you ask a family to leave your school does not mean your relationship must be broken. If you have built a strong relationship, you should be willing to keep the relationship going at a level that makes sense. You should reach out and find out how the family is progressing. Where are they now? Has someone else figured out how to help them succeed? If so, what have they done? Find out what you can learn from this situation to help others in the future. Every experience is a learning experience in early childhood education, especially for teachers.

An early child care program accepts responsibility for all children in its facility. It is your job to provide a safe setting in which children do not need to hurt each other to achieve their ends. Asking children to leave is a difficult decision, but if your program is confident that you have made every effort to help them, they may be served better somewhere else. Your decision is not about kicking children out but about helping their families to move where they and their children will get the help they need to succeed.

OPTIMIZE YOUR KNOWLEDGE

1   What are the limitations that your program may have in helping children with challenging behavior?

_____

_____

_____

_____

_____

2 Have you ever played a part in asking a child to leave the center? Why did you reach that decision? What was difficult about it?

_____

_____

_____

_____

_____

3 Explain why it is occasionally better for children to leave your program.

_____

_____

_____

_____

_____

Early childhood classrooms are full of activity. When challenging behaviors occur in your classroom, you are challenged to maintain a broader perspective and pull together with your team. Many challenging behaviors can be prevented or eased by better classroom management on your part. Others may require additional help, and that's okay too.

Understanding each child can be a challenge at times, and it requires teachers who truly appreciate and like children for what they can do, with all the variations of abilities and temperament found in any group. Keep that in mind when you enter your classroom each day. Children are wonderful people who deserve the best you have to offer.

Certificate of Achievement

This certificate is presented to

_____

for completing the professional development program:

Winning Ways for Early Childhood Professionals: Guiding Challenging Behavior

Gigi Schweikert
www.gigischweikert.com

Redleaf Press®
www.redleafpress.org
800-423-8309

The author and Redleaf Press have not verified the actual completion of the program by this participant.